# The BRULES of life

COMPANION WORKBOOK

15 Bullshit RULES to BREAK for a NO-VACATION-NEEDED Life

TARA SAGE

The Brules of Life Companion Workbook.
Part of The Book of Brules series.


Published by Book Bubble Press
ISBN 9781912494668

 The resources in this book are provided for informational purposes only and should not be used to replace the specialized training and professional judgment of a health care or mental health care professional. Neither the author nor publisher can be held responsible for the use of the information provided within this book. Please, always consult a trained professional before making any decision regarding treatment of yourself or others.

Book Bubble Press

# A SPECIAL GIFT FOR YOU

"An Unconventional 5-minute Dream Acceleration Meditation"



GO TO: www.tarasagecoaching.com/um

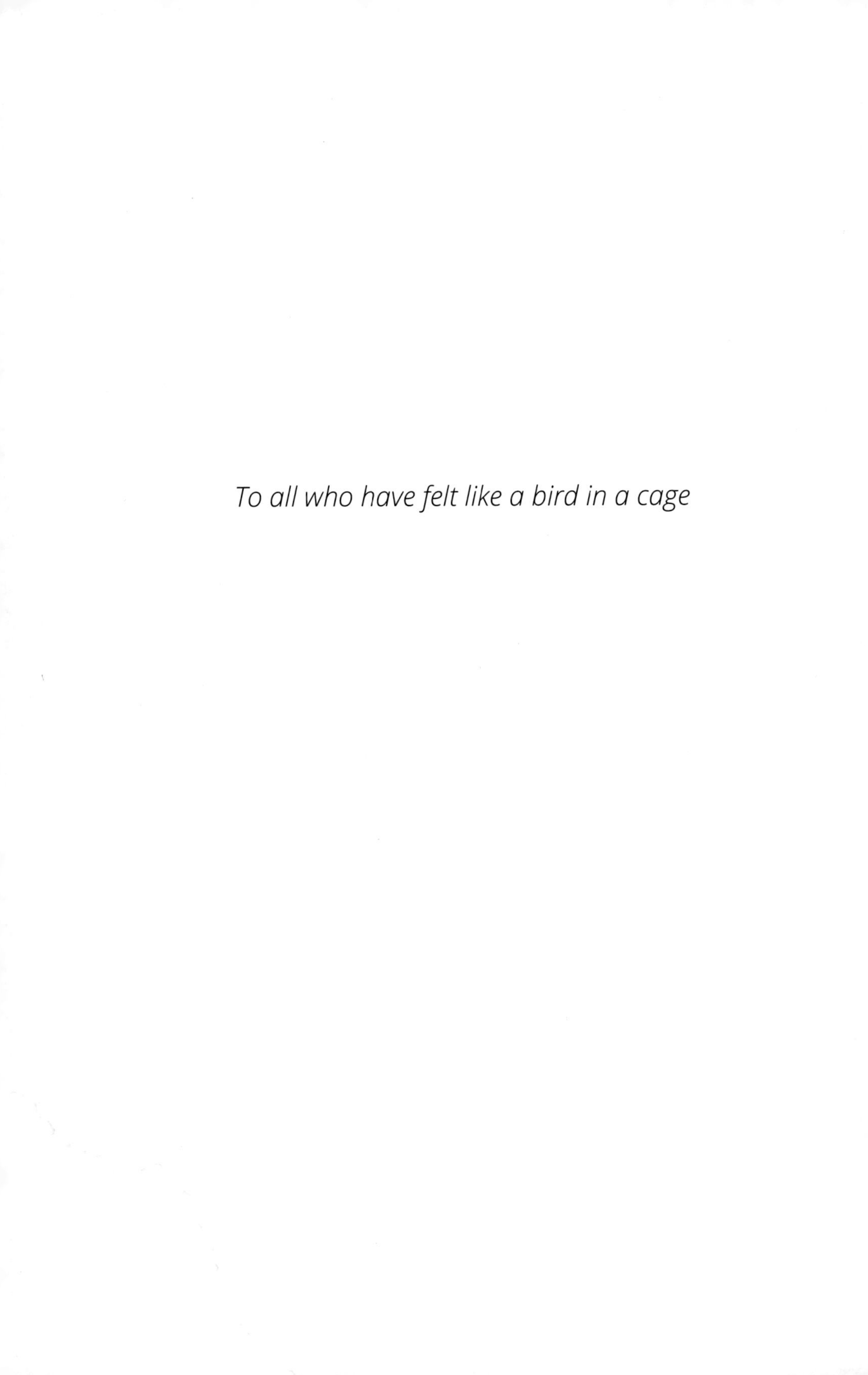

*To all who have felt like a bird in a cage*

Brules

Very few people stop to smell the brules, let alone question them. Since you're holding this companion workbook in your brave hands, clearly, you are not one of those people. Yay, you!

May this companion workbook give you the strategic fuel and supportive structure you need for your own brule-breaking life-enhancing pleasure. In addition to coaching others to do so, I have personally broken every single one of the brules included in *The Brules of Life.* One page at a time, we are going to crack the code on how to be fully and unapologetically yourself, break some brules, put hacks and re-frames to work for you, and change the game on who you get to be and how you get to live. I'm glad to be on this journey with you!

***If you haven't already, please accept my invitation to join my Brule Breakers Club at www.bookofbrules.com. Come for community, stay for the brule-breaking support and banter. It's also where I prerelease new content for future books!***

*Grab a favorite pen, and let's get started!*

Brules often hide in plain sight. How many bullshit rules can you think of? List them here:.

## A Brule of Thumb

Pay attention and stay on the lookout for brules that hide in plain sight.

When a thought, circumstance or idea sparks you to ask (be it silently or out loud) "Is that allowed??" ... explore these questions for a brule-busting breakthrough:

1. What rule would you be breaking? [Be specific.]
2. Who wrote it?
3. Whose voice are you hearing it said in?
4. Is it true?

# Brule #1:
# Better to Be Safe Than Sorry

While not a comfortable truth, no one gets out alive. This can be depressing or it can be the most potent joy juice ever.

Looking back on your life so far, what are some of the most memorable stories that come to mind for you? Write out a few of your most memorable stories.

What stands out to you about what makes the stories memorable or noteworthy? Make some notes here about what you're noticing.

You get to steer your life in the direction of your own choosing and you get to choose how and where to invest your precious energy.

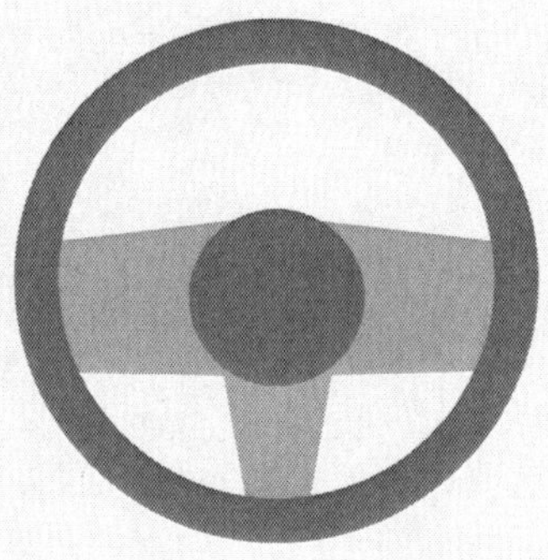

If you are not actively pursuing your dreams, or you're telling yourself "later" or "someday," then by default, you are deciding to live your precious life in a way that treats your dreams like they are not as important as your fears.

#truthbomb

Write down how you know you are living your life on YOUR TERMS and any thoughts about where you see room for improvement. Where do you want to be living MORE on your own terms?

Which of these motivates you more: Doing what you think will get you approval from others, or marching to the beat of your own drum regardless of what others think? How do you know?

Write specific examples that clearly display evidence of this.

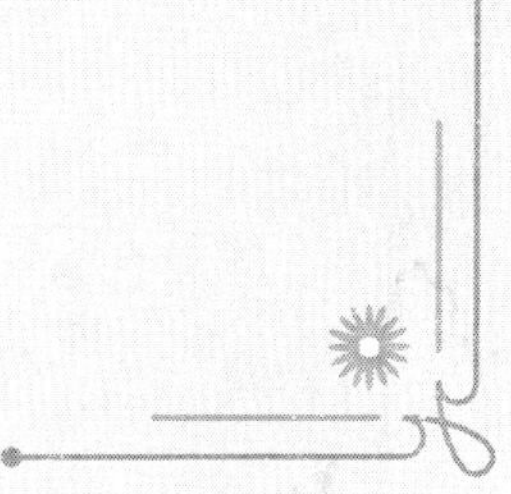

Someday when you're old and gray, sitting in a rocking chair, what are the stories YOU will be telling?

If tomorrow you get caught in a landslide or swooped up by a tornado, would TODAY have been the last day you dreamed of?

*Circle one:*

*Hell yes!* *No, not really.*

Imagine a dream day. Write it out, starting from the moment you wake up, all the way through, to when you lay your head down to sleep. What would an ideal dream day be for YOU?

Describe it here, in as much detail as possible.

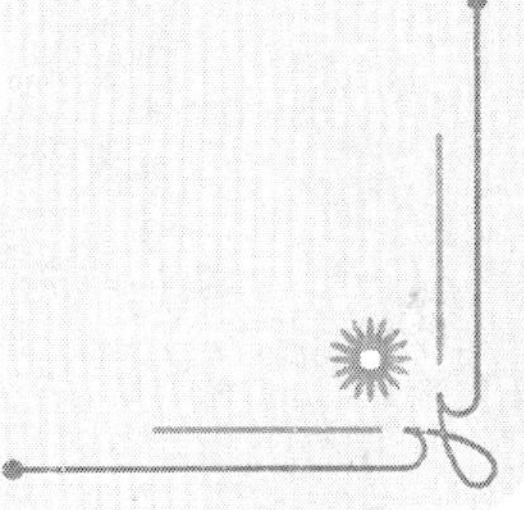

None of us knows how long we have,
so live like you mean it.

Do the things ... because none of us
gets out alive.

Don't play it too safe ... because
regret is a killer.

Don't wait for later ... because
"someday" isn't a day of the week.

**Consider two scenarios and notice where you see yourself in them.**

*Scenario 1:*

Someone you know is doing something bold, new, unconventional, different, taking a risk to pursue a dream, going down a road they haven't gone down before.

Which one are you more inclined to say:

"Look out!" ... or, "Rock on!"?

Recall examples of times you have been a voice of caution or a voice of encouragement. Which voice is generally louder? How do you know?

*Scenario 2:*

Going to see a movie, you enter the theater and notice there are just a few people in line waiting to buy tickets. How do you go about getting in line? Do you double back and forth, back and forth, zig-zagging your way through the maze designed to support a long line of people? Do you follow the implied rule that this is the path to the ticket counter? Or, without hesitation, do you dodge the maze and duck under the barrier to get behind the last person in line because you don't need to herd yourself through a maze when you can clearly see the direct path to the end of the line...?

Which scenario speaks more closely to your instincts?

While these hypothetical scenarios obviously aren't high stakes, what are you noticing about your first inclinations? How do they serve you? How do they impede you?

The cost of NOT following some rules can be profoundly and cumulatively detrimental, both to you and others. And, the cost of blindly following other rules can be profoundly and cumulatively detrimental, both to you and others.

Spotting what's what and which rule *not* to follow can get murky, fast! That is, if you can spot them at all since many of the biggest culprits hide in plain sight.

It's why most people resign themselves to rule-following without question, only to end up paying a high price: costs to their heart, soul, happiness, principles, and well-being (to name a few).

Rather than question or take on rewriting of old assumptions, beliefs, and behaviors, they play it "safe." They stay within the lines. They do what's expected. They follow the path that is presented, whether it makes sense or not.

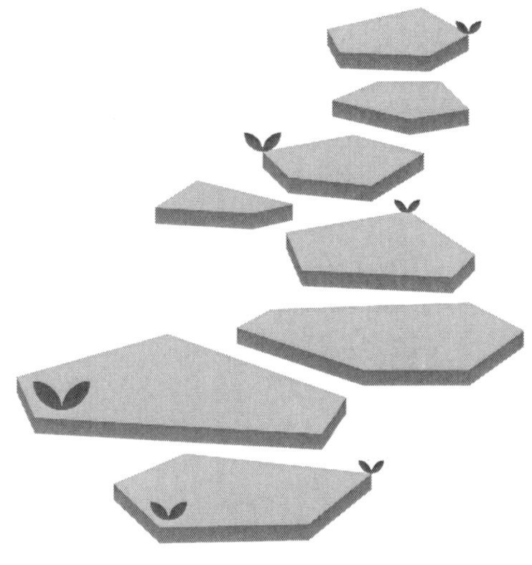

Do an honest inventory: How has playing it safe *cost* you? What opportunities *didn't* you take out of fear or caution?

How might a shift in behavior create a shift in your life? What do you imagine might happen if your rebel soul were to start questioning what you've previously accepted as just the way it is? Write it out.

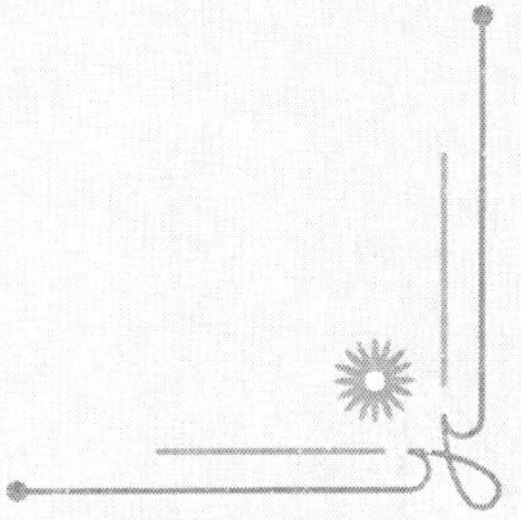

How has playing it safe been detrimental to your happiness?

Where in your life have you grown accustomed to a bit too much of the same-old-same-old?

YOU are in the driver's seat of your life, whether you like it or not.

Take the wheel.

Become your own green light.

Decide that it's go-time, in whatever direction you choose.

Consider that the lines are suggestions, not requirements.

What changes are you looking to make? Be specific.

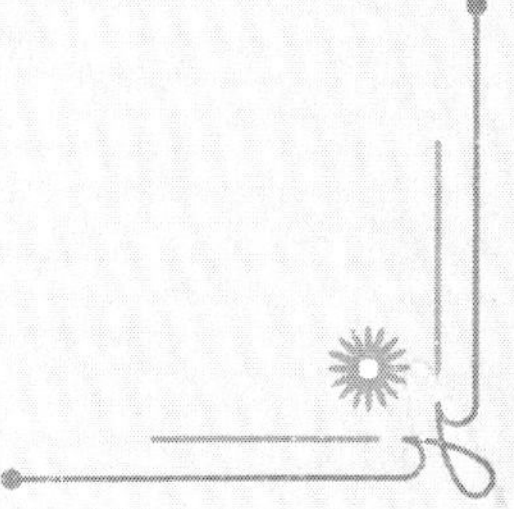

While sometimes change can be big and dramatic, be assured that it doesn't have to be earth shattering to be significant. Sweeping change can make serious waves, but lasting change generally happens incrementally. There's no shame in making small intentional shifts. One advantage of deciding to make small intentional shifts is that such changes are less likely to trigger the "later game."

The key is this: If you want things to be different, do things differently, now.

Since we always create from the present moment, and life is just a string of moments - *now* is your moment. Now is your opening.

Now.

Now.

Now.

What will you do differently today?

Whatever it is that you choose to do differently, allow it to be a symbolic welcoming of new patterns and new experiences in your life. Allow it to serve as a small yet powerful demonstration of your personal willingness to embark on a playful adventure into the unknown.

Pay attention to how it feels to break your usual pattern. Tune in and be the curious observer of your own experience. Really notice what comes up for you, and write down your observations. (Embracing the experiment that is your life, for fun, you might pretend you're wearing a lab coat while making notes.)

*End of day reflections*

What did YOU do differently today? How did it feel?

What did you notice about how set you are in your day-to-day routine?

Did anything surprise you? What did you learn about yourself?

What did you notice about how set you are in your day-to-day routine?

What did you notice about how others responded to your experiment?

How did you respond to their response?

Even the slightest new awareness can fertilize and nourish seeds of change. What one new awareness, however small, did you have today?

As you lay your head on your pillow tonight, do it with the peace of knowing that you are proactively creating your well-lived life.

***A free gift for you: If you haven't already, go now to [www.tarasagecoaching.com/um](www.tarasagecoaching.com/um) to claim your "Unconventional 5-minute Dream Acceleration Meditation" and start today to head in the direction of what you most deeply desire.***

# Brule #2:
# Achieving Goals Makes You Happy

Too often, people set out to achieve goals that don't fit into the bigger picture view of what they truly, deeply want.

When a goal is a silo, reaching it will more than likely feel disappointing, even despairing, despite your "success."

Underwhelming, at the minimum.

Recall a personal example or instance when you achieved a goal that left you feeling anticlimactic lackluster. What did it feel like to "check the box" on a goal your heart wasn't really in?

Describe the experience.

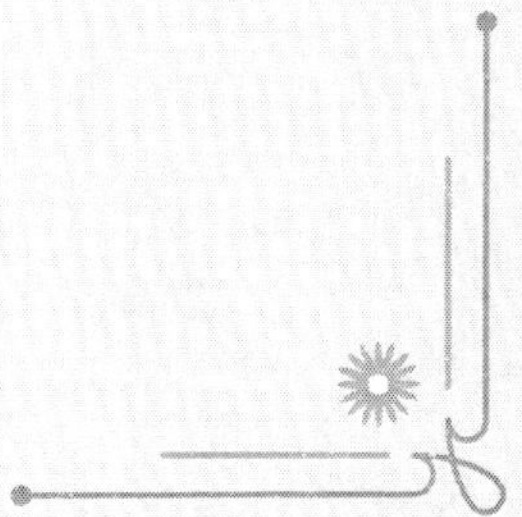

Now, recall a time when you achieved a goal that moved you closer to a deeply held dream. What was *that* experience like?

*Notice the difference. Notice how a goal without a dream is a recipe for dissatisfaction. For fulfillment of a goal to be truly satisfying, it needs to support a dream that excites your soul.*

What dream excites your soul?

Write out and review your current goals in the space below. Which of your current goals support the realization of your deepest dreams? Which don't? Be specific.

What needs to shift so that all your goals align with your dreams?

YOU are the ultimate authority on what you want, so only you can know these answers.

Do what it takes to get clear on this now. Through sincere introspection and honest effort, you're likely to save yourself enormous amounts of time, energy, and perhaps money that you might otherwise spend on the pursuit of anticlimactic goals and lackluster "success."

When you think of it in these terms, seems pretty silly to invest in the pursuit of that which you don't really want, doesn't it?

# Brule #3:
# Don't Get Too Big For Your Britches

Recall a time when you were told you're too much, or "bossy." How did it feel?

If others say you are too much, does it mean you are? Why or why not?

Bring to mind something you avoid or *don't* do in an effort to prevent the possibility of others thinking you're too much. What DON'T you do, as a precaution?

Bring to mind something you purposefully DO in an effort to avert others from thinking you're "too much"? What actions do you take in hopes of preventing such ideas?

Dig deep. In what ways might these actions (or inactions) be self-limiting?

What are your weaknesses?

How might they actually be strengths?

Are you living from your bigness or are you trying to squash it? How do you know?

*A simple, though not necessarily easy, challenge:*

Walk as tall as you are able, everywhere you go.

Claim space and, for crying out loud, please do not say "sorry" to others in your vicinity when you make your way down a hall or through a doorway.

Do NOT apologize for your presence.

Hold the door for others as you wish, but do not *ever* apologize for being in the space with them. To do so implies that they belong but somehow you don't – that their presence is welcomed and allowed, but yours isn't.

Practice giving yourself full permission to be you, as you are.

Claim space like you belong, because you do.

Be you.

The big you.

Sans apology.

# Brule #4:
# Honor Traditions

**Words are powerful.**

"Shoulds" are sneaky.

Few things are actually impossible.

Language awareness can be powerfully transformative.

Fill in the blanks with 10 or more "shoulds":

"I should____________________________________________."

"I should____________________________________________."

"I should____________________________________________."

"I should____________________________________________."

"I should____________________________________________."

"I should____________________________________________."

"I should____________________________________________."

"I should____________________________________________."

"I should____________________________________________."

"I should____________________________________________."

"I should____________________________________________."

"I should____________________________________________."

"I should____________________________________________."

"I should____________________________________________."

"I should____________________________________________."

"I should____________________________________________."

"I should____________________________________________."

List at least 10 things you've believed to be impossible for you:

1. ________________________________________
2. ________________________________________
3. ________________________________________
4. ________________________________________
5. ________________________________________
6. ________________________________________
7. ________________________________________
8. ________________________________________
9. ________________________________________
10. ________________________________________

Then shred it, burn it, or stomp on it as an act of liberation. (Recommended: Use a separate piece of paper so you don't light this book on fire.)

Let this ritual be a declaration, a moment when you decide that from here on out, you, your holidays, and your life are a Should-free Zone.

Repeat this exercise as often as you need to until this brule-breaking declaration is 100% true.

*A simple exercise to reprogram "shoulds":*

As you move through your days, take notice any time you hear yourself say the words "I should." Every time you catch yourself, stop, back up, and restate the sentence. Experiment with replacing the words "I should" with "I could" or "I will."

Rephrase your "should" statements:

"I could/will ________________________________________."

"I could/will ________________________________________."

"I could/will ________________________________________."

"I could/will ________________________________________."

"I could/will ________________________________________."

"I could/will ________________________________________."

"I could/will ________________________________________."

"I could/will ________________________________________."

"I could/will ________________________________________."

"I could/will ________________________________________."

"I could/will ________________________________________."

Read them out loud. Notice how it feels.

What does tradition mean to YOU?

What traditions light you up or feed your soul?

What traditions irritate or annoy you? What traditions or rituals have you outgrown?

Going forward, what actions will you take to ensure that holidays, anniversaries, birthdays, and any other recurring item on your calendar area should-free zone for you?

By eliminating one “should” at a time, know that you are consciously making room in your life for more empowered choices.

Recommended: Only maintain traditions that feel truly aligned, joyful, expansive, relevant, and yummy.

# Brule #5:
# Dreams Are Fleeting

Take a quiet moment now to pause and take a few breaths.

Connect to that place inside you where your deepest dreams and desires reside, where your imagination speaks.

Have a peek. Have a listen.

*Friendly reminder:* You are the ultimate authority on what you want. Noone knows better than you what YOU want.

Own this authority as you respond to the following questions.

What dream has been in your heart for years, if not decades? Declare it here.

What is at the top of YOUR "bucket list"?

What dream makes your heart skip a beat and turns up the brightness on the light within? Write it down.

What dream is waiting for YOU? Name it.

**If you feel clear about what your big dream is, do this:**

Thank your dream.

Thank it for all the ways it nudges you to grow and realize the truth of what you are capable of. Thank it for challenging you to be a bigger bolder full-expression version of yourself.

*Pro tip:* Set aside needing to know how to make it happen, for now. Resist the "how hole."

Just let yourself see it, know it, savor it, and want it – without apology. Believe in your dream, even and especially if you have no clue how to make it so.

**If you *don't* feel clear about what your big dream is, do this:**

Decide that it is time to get clear on what you truly deeply want. In order to create and live a life you love, you must first get clear on what you want. There's simply no way around that.

*Don't worry ...* We've got plenty of hacks, places to look for clues, tools and strategies to help you turn the volume up on your deepest dreams and desires.

If you knew you had one year to live, what would you do to ensure it was a life well lived? Write until you feel the truth of your answer.

What don't you want? Create a big long list. Then "flip" each statement and let your "don't want" list inspire a just-as-long "wants" list.

| *Don't Want* | *Want (Zone of Yes)* |
|---|---|
| | |

| *Don't Want* | *Want (Zone of Yes)* |
| --- | --- |
| | |

If another six months or year goes by without taking action on your dreams, will that be ok with you?

Circle one:

*Yup, totally fine.* *Um, no.*

Consider this: What will be the cost of NOT making a change?

What do you feel envy or jealousy toward others about? What do others have – or appear to have – that sparks jealousy or envy within you? Answering this question can powerfully reveal what you desire.

What do others have that you want? Write it down.

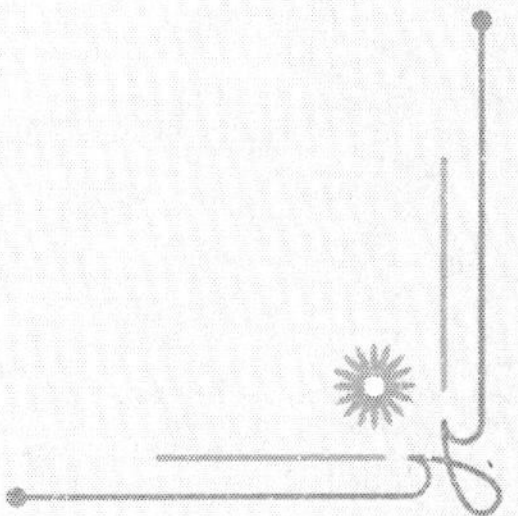

What action will you take in the next 24 hours to move forward on the dreams in your heart?

*Have you claimed the Unconventional 5-minute Dream Acceleration Meditation I recorded to help you tune in, hear the voice of your soul, and listen for the dreams in your heart?*

Claim it now!

An Unconventional 5-Minute Dream Acceleration Meditation for YOU

*www.tarasagecoaching.com/um*

# Brule #6:
# Be Realistic

*"Impossible is not a fact. It's an opinion. Impossible is not a declaration. It's a dare. Impossible is potential. Impossible is temporary. Impossible is nothing."*
*- Muhammad Ali*

Are YOU willing to be surprised by what you're capable of?

*Circle one:* Yes / No

Are you willing to question previously held ideas about what "realistic" means so you can e x p a n d into new possibilities?

*Circle one:* Yes / No

Are you ready to blow the doors open on what's possible?

*Circle one:* Yes / No

Yes? Let's do this thing.

How do you define "realistic"? Write your personal definition here.

Dig deep. What does your current definition of realistic reveal about you?

What is “impossible” daring you to do?

If it was guaranteed to happen and you couldn't fail, what would you pursue?

If you couldn't do it wrong, what would you create?

If you had the full and unwavering support of others, what would you do?

If you had unlimited resources, what problems would you solve?

Allow "realistic" to evolve and expand along with you. The more expanded your view, the greater your ability to believe in possibilities that go beyond what you can see.

What definition of "realistic" are you stretching or growing into?

Imagine: With an expanded definition of "realistic," what might become possible for you? Capture the vision here.

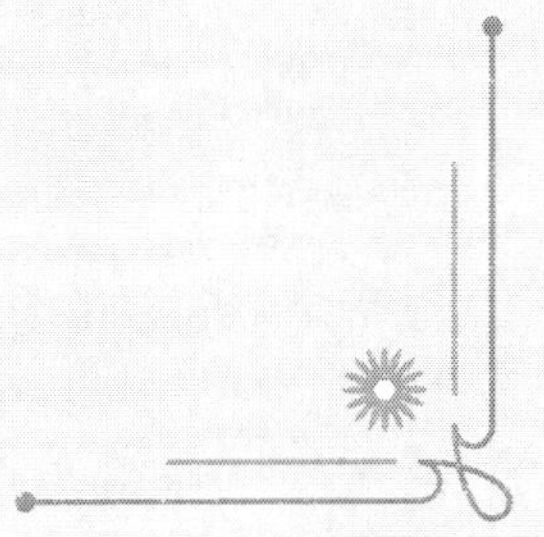

*For a sampling of diverse and inspiring goals and dreams Tara has been able to support clients in creating, visit [www.tarasagecoaching.com/client-stories/](www.tarasagecoaching.com/client-stories/)*

# Brule #7:
# Be Independent

I challenge you to bring to mind one thing you do that is truly independent of all others.

Double check: Are you sure it's *truly and completely* independent? If so, what makes you sure?

Dig deep. What are your current beliefs about independence? Write whatever comes to mind for you.

Which takes precedence in your life – independence or interdependence? How do you know?

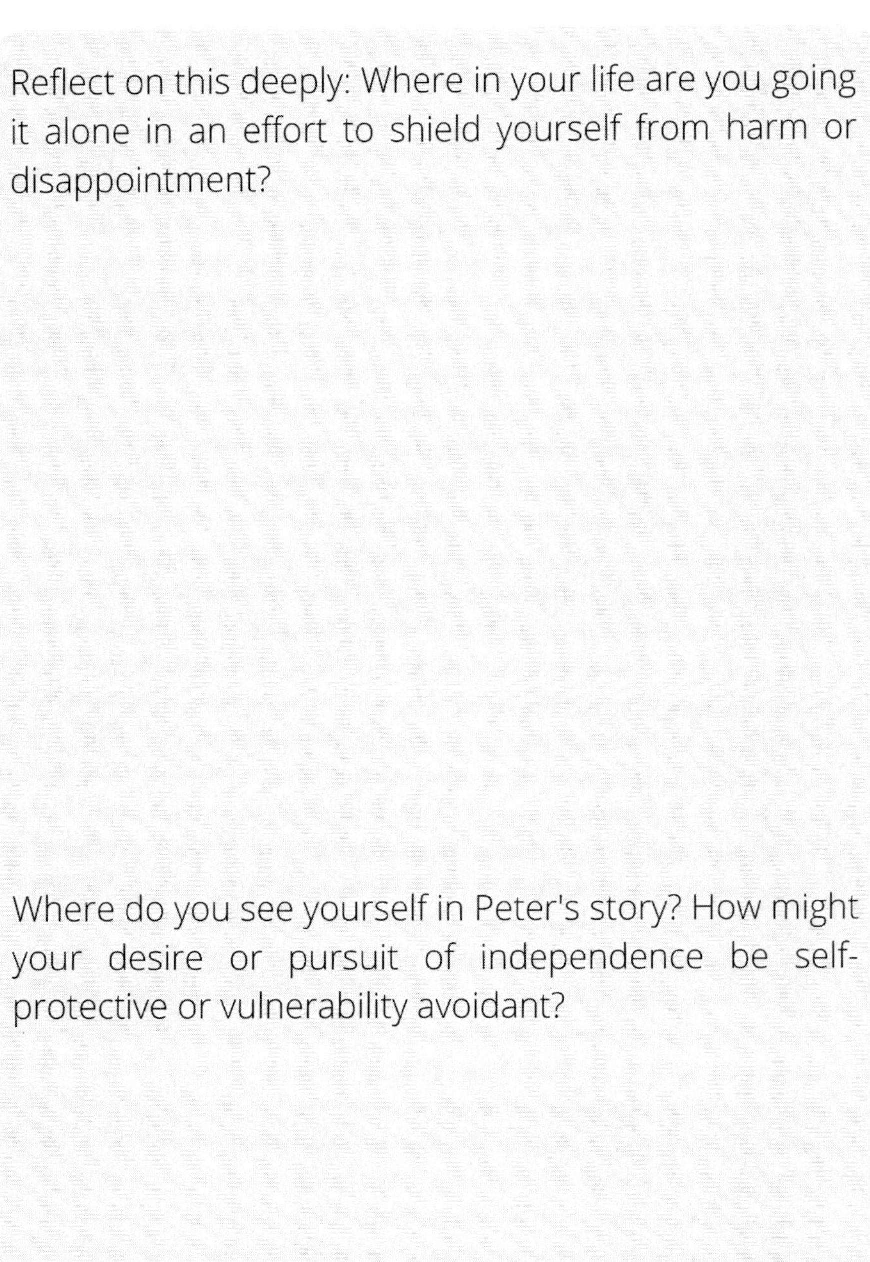

Reflect on this deeply: Where in your life are you going it alone in an effort to shield yourself from harm or disappointment?

Where do you see yourself in Peter's story? How might your desire or pursuit of independence be self-protective or vulnerability avoidant?

How might your desire or pursuit of independence make you difficult to collaborate or connect with?

What can/will you do to strengthen your interdependence muscle? Be specific.

As you practice and embrace interdependence and active collaboration on a new level, what opportunities do you anticipate and/or hope for?

# Brule #8: Wealth is Measured in Dollars

How do YOU define true wealth?

Where do you see yourself in Joanne's story?

Where do you see yourself in Tara's story?

What's your "dining room table"? In the same way that Tara's dining room table challenged her, consider: What do YOU have that you don't want to leave or let go of? What makes you want to hold on or stay put, literally or figuratively?

Explore the “paradox of less”: How might having less "stuff" support you in having more "stuff of life"?

What do you want more of in your life?

What has you holding on, staying put, or feeling weighed down?

*A powerful, two-part downsizing strategy:*

(1) Start with one drawer, and two questions. Open a drawer and take everything out. Sort through each thing, one item at a time and ask yourself:

Do I NEED it?
Do I LOVE it?

Be diligent. If you cannot answer with a resounding "Yes" to at least one of these two questions, out it goes. Buh-bye.

Where to? Well, pick one:

- Trash or recycle bin
- Donation to a local charity
- Gift it to someone you know who needs and/or would love it.
- Sell it (consignment, craigslist, letgo, yard sale, etc.)

Repeat.

One drawer at a time, until you're done with drawers. Then open a cabinet, one shelf at a time. Take on one contained space at a time, piecemeal.

(2) Before bringing any more *stuff* into your world, dig deep and ask:

- Why do you want the things you want?
- What is the experience you are truly seeking?

The answers may be enlightening.

Such questions can be a window into your deepest personal values and priorities.

It's a discovery process that can reveal powerful insights into your sense of meaning, purpose, and fulfillment.

Use this space to write about whatever is surfacing for you:

What do you want when you're not striving for the things you've been told you "should" want? (Let your inner wisdom flow…)

# Brule #9: It'll Happen When the Time is Right

*"Everything happens Now. You remember your past Now. You dream your future Now. You learn from your past Now. When you were actually in your past, it was still Now. At that point in the past, if someone were to ask you what you were doing now, it would still be Now. You work toward your future Now. You will get to your future Now. You will live in your future Now. You are always Here, Now. You cannot Be anywhere else. Being, Is-ness, is only Now. There is nothing you can do in any other moment except Now. Try it. Do something yesterday or tomorrow right now. Impossible! You can only Be and Do Now. It is all Now. Even "tomorrow" is happening Now, is Now."*

*- David Cameron Gikandi*

What dream(s) or goal(s) in your heart *haven't* you pursued?

Why haven't you?

Consider that the time is right as soon as you decide it is.

What decision are you making, once?

*Ready for kind caring support and no-BS guidance on your side as you blaze your own trail and successfully create a life you feel proud of and delighted by? If you're ready to show up for new possibilities, make today YOUR someday, and create a new kind of experience of life, get started today at www.tarasagecoaching.com.*

# Brule #10: Don't Blow Out Your Friend's Birthday Candles

Kidding. This is totally a rule to live by.

As is, making a big, bold, audacious wish when you blow out your own candles.

Truth is you can make big, bold, audacious wishes anytime.

What are you wishing for?

# Brule #11:
# You Must Go to Work

What in your life can you apply the mantra "for now, not forever" too?

Recall a time you felt like you were wearing a costume or playing a role meant for someone else. Describe the feeling in your own words.

Awareness is powerful. Make note of any area(s) of your life that currently feel like you're playing a part meant for someone else?

What one action will you take in the next 24 hours to move forward on hacking the way you work? Be specific.

# Brule #12: Root Where You Are Planted

Muse on this:

Who would YOU be, if no one knew who you were?

*"If you don't like how things are, change it. You're not a tree." Jim Rohn*

What has travel taught you about yourself?

Do you feel you have traveled far enough to meet yourself? Why or why not?

Where would YOU like to go?

Star or circle the top one or two places you would love to go to.

Hold the picture in your mind's eye. Engage your senses as you see, feel, and imagine it: your journey, your style, your way.

Use this space to describe the experience:

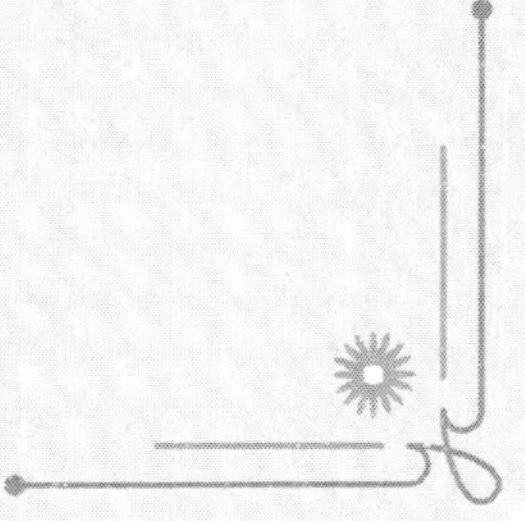

What are you longing for?

How do you define "home"?

## Ever said any of these things?

*Check any that apply.*

___ "I'll travel more, someday."
___ "I'll spend more time in nature, soon."
___ "I'll work less – right after x, y, z project is done."
___ "I'll take better care of myself, tomorrow."
___ "I'll nurture my relationships more, soon."
___ "I'll bring on more support, someday."
___ "I'll simplify my life, next week."
___ "I'll create more order and have less stuff, soon."
___ "I'll have more free time – after x, y, z, and a, b, c is done."

Rather than "maybe someday" what action(s) are you taking to make *today* the someday you've been waiting for?

***Ready to really learn the ins and outs of how to live nomadically – for a month, a season, a year or forever? In Nomadic Living 101, we show you how. Learn how to make this lifestyle your own with actionable steps and practical advice from people who are committed to not only answering all the questions we know you have (because we had them too), but also answer all the questions you don't know to ask (it's hard to find answers to questions that you don't know you don't know). Visit www.nomadicliving101.com for details and support on all things logistical, mechanical, lifestyle and social.***

# Brule #13:
# Make New Year Resolutions

Regardless of what time of year it happens to be, stop and consider:

What "season" is it for YOU? Is it a time to plant? A time to reap? A time to cast away? Or perhaps, a time for gathering stones together?

Use this space to explore these questions:

*A time-off hack:*

Sit down with your calendar and schedule time off for the next twelve months, now. While you're at it, mark your calendar to do it again nine months from now so you are always scheduling time off at least three months ahead.

*Looking back*

Reflect on the last twelve, six, or three months. Create a great big long list, or a short list (up to you), of things that you've accomplished, created or are appreciative about.

What dreams, goals, or resolutions did NOT come to fruition for you?

*Looking forward*

What do you REALLY want to experience?

How do you want this year to be different from last year? What changes would you like to see? What is your heart longing for more of? What is your heart longing for less of? Be specific.

Name five “buckets” or significant areas of your life:

Decide on three to five specific, measurable goals for each. Write them in the spaces below.

Bucket ______________________________

Bucket ______________________________

Bucket ______________________________

Bucket ______________________________

Bucket ______________________________

As you create your "buckets" and identify your goals for each, tune in to what is at the heart of your intentions.

One key aspect of successful resolutions is knowing your "why." Check to be sure it's not a "should" or something someone else wants for you, but what you *truly* want.

## *Top 10 lists*

Top 10 lists are a fun way to bring focus to your intentions, joys, and desires.

Enjoy making your unique-as-you lists:

### Top 10 Things I Love about My Life

## Top 10 Moments from This Year

## Top 10 Priorities for the Coming Year

## Top 10 Ways I Spread Light in The World

## Top 10 Things That Are Uniquely "Me"

## Top 10 Books I Want to Read

## Top 10 Things I'd Like to Do Before I Die

## Top 10 Reasons for Gratitude in My Life

## Top 10 Things I Want to Learn

## Top 10 Activities That Make Me Feel Alive

..............................................................................................................

..............................................................................................................

..............................................................................................................

..............................................................................................................

..............................................................................................................

..............................................................................................................

..............................................................................................................

..............................................................................................................

..............................................................................................................

..............................................................................................................

What stands out to you about your Top 10 lists?

Dig deep. Get to the heart of the matter: Why do you want what you want? Write out your reasons, even if they seem obvious.

By clarifying your "why" at the start, in the event that you get off track, you'll be able to more quickly reconnect to your "why" fuel. Why is a touchstone, a reminder, a recharge station for when change feels hard - and it undoubtedly will. By getting clear about “the whys” behind each of your goals, you’ll more easily be able to stay the course.

Complete each sentence to further activate and fuel your authentic motivation:

1.) "This year I will ______________ because ..." *or* "I resolve to _________ because ..."

2.) "When I successfully accomplish this, I will ..."

3.) "If I give up or don't follow through, I will ..."

Good job! To take it even further, rate the strength of your desire for each goal on a scale of 1-10.

| *Your goal* | *Your "why"* | *1-10 rating* |
|---|---|---|
| | | |

| *Your goal* | *Your "why"* | *1-10 rating* |
|---|---|---|
| | | |

Psst ... If you've rated the strength of your desire for any goal as less than 7 out of 10, consider adding it to the fuck-its bin and focus on the things that have serious juice.

Which goals, if any, do you see belong in the fuck-its bin? List them here:

Goals that help you survive tend to bring a sense of relief and necessity. Goals that help you thrive tend to be enriching and expansive. Neither is wrong or bad or less than valid or important. What are you noticing about your goals? Make some notes here:

A cherry on top! Decide on a "word of the year," write a statement of intent - or both! Choose a word or theme that lights you up when you say it.

*(Stay alert for "shoulds" and "fuck-its" wanting to sneak their way in.)*

"My word of the year is ______________________."

"I declare that my life feels ____________________. The energies of ______________________ empower and fuel __________________________________."

Feel free to use this space to create a vision board, doodle, or paste magazine images that speak to the "vibe" you intend to create.

## Your action plan

Last but certainly not least, create a supportive action plan for how to move forward toward your desired outcomes.

What are you going to *do* differently in the coming year than you did last year? What will you *do* on behalf of each goal you've set?

(e.g: "I resolve to ______________________ on behalf of my desire for _______________________________.")

Good plans include built-in accountability and what I like to refer to as a “Dream Team” of support.

Accountability breeds responsibility.

Your commitment to action tends to deepen or be reinforced when you’ve declared it to others who have the expectation that you can and will succeed. We all have our lone ranger tendencies, but the right support really does make all the difference.

Who is on YOUR Dream Team? How does each individual support you?

Having a skilled coach on your side can help you stay on track, overcome the hurdles, navigate your unique version of sabotage psychology, and ensure that you succeed at what you are setting out to create.

Who (else) would you like to have on your Dream Team?

***Want me on your Dream Team? Join my signature coaching program! The Dream Acceleration Program is a very special program and journey that has not only life-changing, dream-propelling content, but also built-in accountability coaching sessions to support you in full implementation of the material on behalf of your dream life. Learn all about it and claim your seat at www.dreamaccelerationprogram.com.***

# Brule #14: Eliminate Fear

*"The fears we don't face become our limits."*
*- Robin Sharma*

What would YOU do if you weren't afraid?

The presence of fear does not mean that you don't have what it takes. Quite the contrary! Fear is jet fuel for your best life. It can unleash your potential and launch you forward in unimaginable ways.

Name any and all fears that are holding you back or that you sense are slowing down your success. (e.g. "I see you fear of ________.")

It is understandable to want to avoid fear. But unless you are being chased by a tiger (in which case, run!), consider this: Fear is good news.

Fear is an invitation. Fear is daring you to be a bigger and bolder version of yourself. Fear is high-octane fuel. Fear can propel you forward beyond your wildest dreams. Fear is an invitation, not for avoidance, but for bravely stepping up to the plate and willingly meeting your potential.

How might exposure to what you're afraid of help you develop tolerance for it? How can you apply this strategy to help you do what you are currently afraid to do?

Who's winning - you or fear? How do you know?

Where has fear found its way into the driver's seat of your life?

Take a deep breath and decide on at least one courageous action you will take to move forward on the life you've imagined.

***Fear is tricky. More often than not people find that they need more support. In the Dream Acceleration Program there are special modules designed to help you go deeper with this process, to not just address but s-t-r-e-t-c-h beyond every possible kind of fear. Learn more at www.dreamaccelerationprogram.com.***

# Brule #15:
# You Need a Vacation

Using your imagination can create great things.

The human brain's innate capacity for imagination allows us to envision, anticipate, dream, innovate, strategize and problem solve in ways that other species aren't capable of to the same degree human beings are.

How you use this ability matters, a lot.

Imagine … everyday life being so affirming, gratifying, and joy-filled that you don't need a vacation.

Imagine … there's no need or desire for escape, so if you do take a "vacation" there won't be an ounce of dread or remorse when it's time to return.

Imagine that! No, I mean it. Take a moment now and imagine what that would be like.

What are you envisioning?

Worry is as much an act of imagining as dreaming is. Rather than focus on worry, you can choose to focus on joy.

Let's blow the lid off your joy ceiling!

How much joy can YOU stand? Where do you pull back awkwardly from joy, unsure how to manage, or trust, that much of a good thing? What are you noticing about your current joy ceiling?

*Raise the roof!*

1.) What does survival mode feel like to you? Describe it below.

2.) How much of your survival-ism is currently born of necessity? Be specific. What basic needs are currently being unmet?

3.) How much of your survival-ism is currently born of habit? Give examples of thoughts or behaviors you notice within yourself that continue due to habit, not necessity.

4.) Imagine “thrival mode.” What do you imagine it will feel like to thrive fully? Describe it here.

5.) Dig deep. What do your answers to the previous four questions reveal to you?

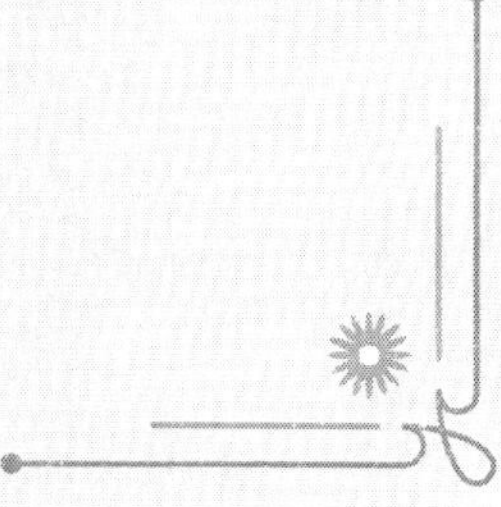

Overflow and simplicity, together, make "thrival" possible.

Where in your life could you benefit from more simplicity? Create a great big long list.

What would it feel like to have these areas of your life simplified? Describe the feeling in your own words.

What would a "hell yes" life look like for you? Describe it in as much detail as you can.

*Let's explore the possibilities together.*
*Visit www.tarasagecoaching.com for details.*

# Bonus Content!

# The Wheel of Self-Actualization

In *The Brules of Life,* Brule #5: Dreams Are Fleeting, we touch on 'The Zone of Yes.' Enjoy this bonus content to help you expand the other three Zones of Clarity!

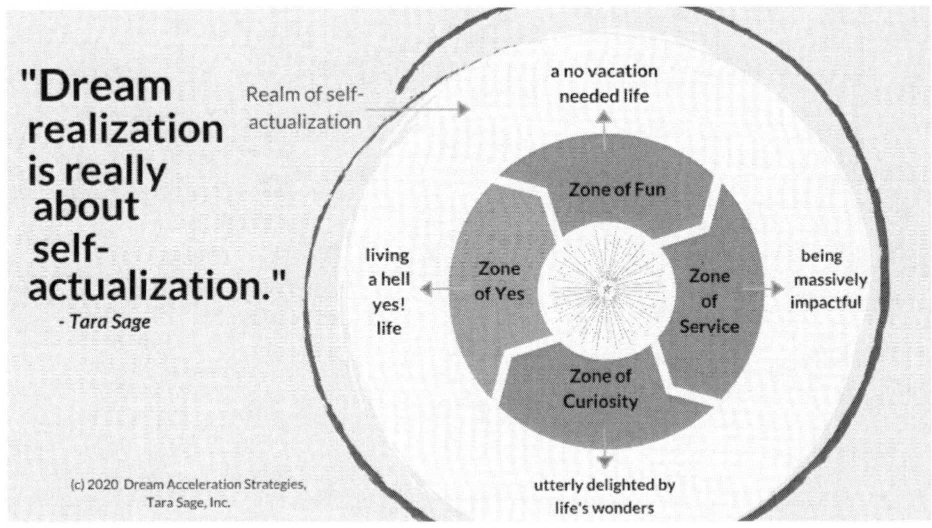

*The Zone of Fun*

Make a list of activities that are fun for you and keep it on hand, especially for all that time-off you claimed on your calendar! What's on your fun list?

*The Zone of Curiosity*

Intellectual curiosity is one avenue to reveal aspects of your dream life. Curiosity feeds the soul. It also provides a mirror for your interests. Your curiosity instincts are as unique as you are.

What intrigues YOU? What are you curious to learn more about? Make a list!

Respond to the following prompts.

I've always wanted to learn how to ...

I'm curious to know more about ...

If I could be a student forever, I'd want to study ...

Things I research in my spare time are ...

I'm totally intrigued by ...

I often wonder about ...

In a bookstore, I gravitate toward ....

I love wandering my way into ______________________ and talking to the people I meet about ...

If I were to have a private "think week" retreat, a week all to myself just for thinking, reading, reflecting, and contemplating, I'd ...

*The Zone of Service*

Service includes YOU. This is so important to understand. Service is sustainable because it feeds your energy while you are serving others.

Brainstorm for insights:

What can you do all day, every day, and never get tired?

What's a problem you want to solve?

Whose plight do you get fired up about?

Who do you want to help?

Who do you want to support and make a difference for?

Who are you passionate about helping?

What acts of service also serve YOU?

Use this space to summarize your insights and discoveries about your Zone of Fun, Zone of Curiousity and Zone of Service.

*To learn more about how Tara might support you in creating a no-vacation-needed life, visit* www.tarasagecoaching.com *for details.*

*Last but not least ...*

## A Letter to Your Future Self

Enter the virtual Time Machine and write a letter to your Future You. Write as if it's five years into the future and you are reflecting on all that you've created, experienced, and achieved over these last five years.

Date: __________

(e.g. If today is May 2022, date your letter May 2027.)

*I am so happy and grateful now that....*

*The first steps I took were...*

Love,

PS – You're awesome.

## Please & Thank You

Thank you for buying and reading this special *Brules of Life Companion Workbook*. I hope you've filled the pages, and enjoyed and benefited from doing so.

If you did ... PLEASE, pretty please, share your thoughts in an Amazon REVIEW. If you gained thought-provoking inspiration, helpful pointers, and actionable strategies from reading *The Brules of Life* and using this *Brules of Life Companion Workbook*, please let others know.

Here are several ways you can do so:

#1: Leave a review on Amazon
#2: Leave a review at Goodreads
#3: Tell your people about it on your Blog, Podcast, E-zine, or YouTube Channel
#4: Share it on Facebook, Instagram, Twitter, Pinterest, or LinkedIn
#5: Mention it to your friends, family and colleagues

Reviews on Amazon are incredibly helpful – both for future readers and for authors like myself to get the word out. Please know that your support is sincerely and deeply appreciated! Thanks again for taking the time!

Love,
Tara Sage

## Appendix/Resources

For ease, here are the resource links mentioned in *The Brules of Life,* all in one place:

- Please accept my invitation to join my Brule Breakers Club at www.bookofbrules.com. Come for community, stay for the brule-breaking support and banter. It's also where I prerelease new content for future books.

- Ready for kind caring support and no-BS guidance as you blaze your own trail and successfully create a life you feel proud of and delighted by? If you're ready to show up for new possibilities, make today YOUR someday, and create a new kind of experience of life, get started today at www.tarasagecoaching.com.

- Want to learn the ins and outs of how to live nomadically – for a month, a season, a year or forever? In Nomadic Living 101, we show you how. Visit www.nomadicliving101.com for details and support on all things logistical, mechanical, lifestyle and social. The freedom of the road awaits!

- Listen to my pre-recorded 'Unconventional 5-minute Dream Acceleration Meditation.' It will help you tune in, hear the voice of your soul, and listen for the dreams in your heart. www.tarasagecoaching.com/um

- To learn all about The Dream Acceleration Program, my signature coaching program, and claim your seat, head on over to www.dreamaccelerationprogram.com.

- Go to www.rainbowfinderapp.com to download Carl's RainbowFinder™ app - never miss a rainbow!

- To read a sampling of the incredibly diverse and inspiring goals and dreams I've been able to support clients in creating, go to www.tarasagecoaching.com/client-stories/

- Want to improve your public speaking confidence, presence, and skills? Check out The Speak Up Program at www.speakupprogram.com.

- For all other Tara Sage Coaching programs and free offers, visit www.tarasagecoaching.com and have a look around.

Last but not least, if you gained thought-provoking inspiration, helpful pointers, and actionable strategies from reading *The Brules of Life*, please tell others about it and leave a review on Amazon and Goodreads.

Thank you!

Additional Space for Notes & Inspiration

Made in United States
North Haven, CT
21 October 2021